T0284791

150 BEST NEW INTERIOR DESIGN IDEAS

150 BEST NEW INTERIOR DESIGN IDEAS

MACARENA ABASCAL VALDENEBRO

HARPER
DESIGN

An Imprint of HarperCollins Publishers

150 BEST NEW INTERIOR DESIGN IDEAS
Copyright © 2021 by LOFT Publications

All rights reserved. No part of this book may be used or reproduced in any manner whatsoever
without written permission, except in the case of brief quotations embodied in critical articles and reviews.
For information, address Harper Design, 195 Broadway, New York, NY 10007.

HarperCollins books may be purchased for educational, business, or sales promotional use.
For information, please email the Special Markets Department at SPsales@harpercollins.com.

First published in 2021 by
Harper Design
An Imprint of *HarperCollins*Publishers
195 Broadway
New York, NY 10007
Tel.: (212) 207-7000
Fax: (855) 746-6023
harperdesign@harpercollins.com
www.hc.com

Distributed throughout the world by
*HarperCollins*Publishers
195 Broadway
New York, NY 10007

Editorial coordinator: Claudia Martínez Alonso
Art director: Mireia Casanovas Soley
Editor and texts: Macarena Abascal Valdenebro
Layout: Cristina Simó Perales

ISBN 978-0-06-299516-2

Library of Congress Control Number: 2020043099

Printed in Malaysia
Second printing, 2021

CONTENTS

INTRODUCTION

It is undeniable that housing is an element that reveals the different social evolutions. Architecture has evolved over time to adapt to changes in our way of life. Modern interior design is a faithful reflection of this. The interiors of houses are the expression of our way of living and working. Functionality, aesthetics, and harmony are closely linked; it is a matter of bringing together the practical needs and the aesthetic aspirations of those who will live in the space. A home must be a sign of identity for those who live in it.

Changes in our way of life as well as in family units give rise to open houses in which spaces are designed to flow into others, and, in some cases, can change their distribution through doors or sliding panels. This promotes greater social interaction by eliminating the visual barriers to give way to open rooms where only the strictly necessary walls are preserved.

The kitchen has, in most cases, become the center of the dwelling, a space in which to cook, receive, and enjoy. It has gone from being a marginal space to a modern space that shares design and aesthetics with the rest of the house.

On the other hand, the bathroom has gone from being just a functional corner to a luminous space where functionality, technology, and design come together to offer an infinite universe of decorative possibilities. The new concept of the bathroom speaks to us of environments with a spa soul. Straight lines are enhanced and the decorations are reduced so as not to overload the environment but to create a peaceful atmosphere in which to enjoy the ritual of bathing or a revitalizing shower.

Contemporary design is no longer as rigorous in the search for a pure, almost aseptic aesthetic, free of all artifice, as was the minimalism of years ago. Spaces are still created with a predominance of simplicity enriched with contrasting styles, textures, materials, and colors, but always in search of harmony.

This book does not intend to be a decalogue of compulsory rules for decoration, but simply to show, through housing projects of diverse typology, carried out by renowned designers and architects, different ideas, decoration tips, and creative and inspiring solutions for different rooms that can be very useful if we embark on the exciting task of decorating what will be our home.

Vista Tower

5,500 sq ft

Chicago, Illinois, United States

Axis Mundi

© Roman Syzonenko

Vista Tower, designed by Studio Gang, is a 101-story, 1,191 ft skyscraper built in Chicago, Illinois. It is the third tallest building on the skyline. Vista's full-floor Sky 360 Penthouses take luxury to another level. Rising from the 76th floor, these magnificent residences command uninterrupted 360-degree views across downtown Chicago and beyond. The architecture and design firm Axis Mundi designed this penthouse in which designer furnishings, limited editions, and important contemporary art create a dazzling space for a contemporary art collector. Known for his glamorous rock star sensibility, designer John Beckmann created a magnum opus that is refined, raw, and understated.

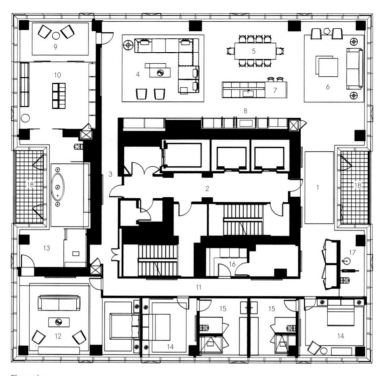

Floor plan

1. Main entry gallery
2. Vestibule
3. West gallery
4. Living area
5. Dining
6. Lounge
7. Island
8. Kitchen
9. Sitting area
10. Wardrobe
11. Private gallery
12. Master bedroom
13. Master bathroom
14. Guest bedroom
15. Guest wardrobe/wc
16. AV/IT, storage, and laundry
17. Powder room
18. Terrace

As you enter, you are surprised by the spectacular views that serve as a backdrop for a modern and elegant ensemble where a corten steel sculpture signed by Tony Cragg undoubtedly takes the leading role.

001

The open living area highlights
a spacious composition of the
Wing seating system designed by
Antonio Citterio and offers the
perfect vantage point from which
to admire one of the most famous
word paintings created by US artist
Christopher Wool.

WANT
TOBE
YOUR
DOG

002

Custom-designed bronze fittings and hardware were specifically designed to contrast with some of the more brutalist concrete textures of the project.

The master bedroom features antique leather sling chairs by Jacques Quinet, a bronze Quark table by Emmanuel Babled, a curvy organic sofa by Domeau & Pérès, and suspended light fixtures by Vincenzo De Cotiis. The space is further enhanced by an exceptional Agnes Martin painting.

The master bathroom is lined with hot-rolled steel panels as well as floating monumental marble and hammered brass vanities, counterposed against a honey onyx divider. The bathtub was custom designed and fabricated from a single block of CNC-milled statuary white marble.

Gran Via

3,121 sq ft
Madrid, Spain

**Ruiz Velázquez
architecture & design**

© Nacho Uribe Salazar

This project consists of the transformation of some old offices into a house in an emblematic building in the center of Madrid. An innovative house, it was inspired by the business character of the owner and his specific needs of functionality.

The refurbishment meant a total transformation of the space, but it maintains the original industrial essence. The architect has carried out this special transformation through an enveloping contrast of white planes and natural wood surfaces, a combination with which he plays, repeats, and differentiates in all the spatial discourse that runs through each room, always with a unitary conception and continuity of space.

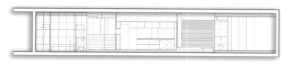

Section 1-1

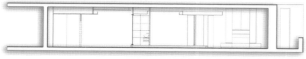

Section 2-2

Section 3-3

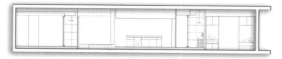

Section 4-4

The reorganization of the floor plan and the distribution of the house are expanded from the inside to the outside by means of three central axes, or differentiated and connected corridors. The resulting space maintains the privacy of each room and is broadly connected by its passages, which are bathed in natural light from the interior of the courtyards.

Floor plan

1. Entrance
2. Hallway
3. Kitchen hallway
4. Living room
5. Bar
6. Kitchen
7. Master bedroom
8. Walk-in closet
9. Master bathroom
10. Bedroom
11. Bathroom
12. Toilet
13. Service entrance
14. Laundry

003

The first corridor enjoys the presence of two large windows with historical black framing, which breaks the aesthetics and connects the space with its origins and with its continent, filling the entrance with light.

004

Lighting directed from the ground enhances the scenery and the three-dimensional effects by breaking planes and highlighting walls with new and different effects.

005

A wooden lattice separates the kitchen from the entrance corridor, but as it is not closed, it allows the light to pass and does not break the spatial continuity. The marble bar becomes, on the inside, a functional piece of furniture designed with the warmth of wood—a practical counter that allows one to attend openly to the dining room as well as the living room.

006

The main area is a continuous space that extends horizontally and parallel to all the light offered by the facade and its windows. The kitchen is located on the opposite side of this platform, elevated as if in an inverted box that allows for a privileged visibility and acts as a room divider.

The master suite has three different areas: the bedroom and bathroom, which feature a primarily white palette, and a dressing room between them built of wood, reproducing the same element of natural compactness and warmth that is used in all other rooms.

007

Warm wooden planes are modulated to create headboards, wardrobes, and hidden doors. They differentiate the various uses of the shared spaces, such as bathroom areas integrated into the rooms or dressing rooms.

Po Shan

2,800 sq ft including balcony
Hong Kong, China

Peggy Bels
© Eugene Chan

The owners of this apartment wanted to renovate it to give it a contemporary look and open up the living and dining areas to increase the feeling of spaciousness.

The designer managed to cleverly join the common areas, despite the existing structural beam, which, when covered with the same finish as the walls, far from appearing to be an obstacle, became an interesting divider of the room without losing the feeling of openness.

The contrast of materials creates an incredible sense of dynamism in a home that has become an ideal place to enjoy moments of rest, leisure, and family fun.

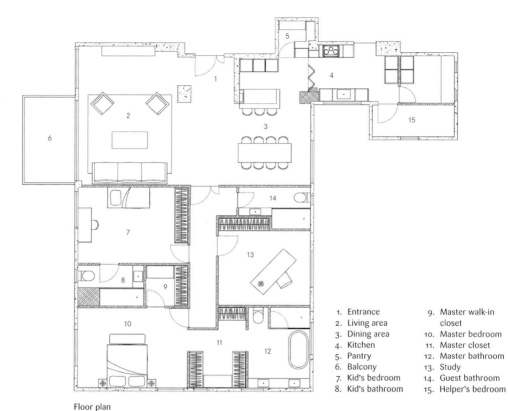

Floor plan

1. Entrance
2. Living area
3. Dining area
4. Kitchen
5. Pantry
6. Balcony
7. Kid's bedroom
8. Kid's bathroom
9. Master walk-in closet
10. Master bedroom
11. Master closet
12. Master bathroom
13. Study
14. Guest bathroom
15. Helper's bedroom

008

The kitchen was opened to the dining room through an island, and the entrance to the living area was opened by removing a wall, thus increasing the feeling of spaciousness. The master bedroom was also opened to a large bathroom and an exposed dressing room.

009

The walls of the living room and
the dining room are finished with
a mixture of cement and a little
water that gives them a milky tone
that is warm and welcoming.

010

Wooden furnishings soften the
severity of the industrial materials.
In the dining room, a wooden
dining table and matching Norman
Cherner chairs from Lane Crawford
add a sense of warmth.

011

The open, airy breakfast bar and dining area are marked by custom-made black metal cabinetry and a slick marble countertop. These dark backgrounds allow the light colors to pop, creating more contrast and depth.

Entering through the corridor that leads to the private areas, on the left is the study and TV room, furnished with a vintage loveseat.

012

The private area—master bedroom, dressing room, and children's room—shares the palette of materials with the rest of the house. However, it has been enriched with fabrics, decorative accessories, and bedding that add notes of color and create a more intimate and cozy atmosphere.

This penthouse is located in the emblematic Eixample district of Barcelona, overlooking the Sagrada Familia temple. The premise of the clients—of Dutch origin—when tackling the renovation project was to maintain the essence of the property, but at the same time to be a modern home, with the necessary technology to obtain maximum comfort.

As a result, they obtained an elegant, modern, and at the same time timeless home, with clean and balanced spaces, where the Barcelona charm of the past coexists in perfect harmony with the modernity of the present.

Passeig Sant Joan

3,713 sq ft
Barcelona, Spain

Abrils Studio

© Montse Garriga

013

The house had huge concrete pillars that were replaced by slender cast-iron ones with a concrete base, typical of Barcelona, which were purchased from an antique shop.

Living room detail

014

A floating oak staircase links the living area with the loft. As it is embedded in the wall, it does not take away space and, because of its design, adds visual interest to the room.

015

White is the common thread of the whole project. This sobriety was broken with a palette of bright and warm colors in all the rooms in order to achieve balance and harmony throughout the house.

Some of the existing elements were preserved, such as the herringbone parquet, which was polished and varnished. It was combined with the black-and-white hydraulic floors, typical of the houses in Barcelona's Eixample district. As the original floors were very deteriorated, they were exchanged for new ones, with a very similar design, and combined with another model of new flooring, also in black and white.

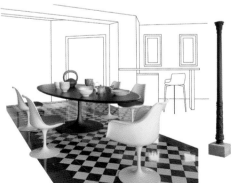

Dining room detail

016

To cover the kitchen floor, the same hydraulic tile was used as in the dining room, so if the sliding door is open, both rooms are integrated.

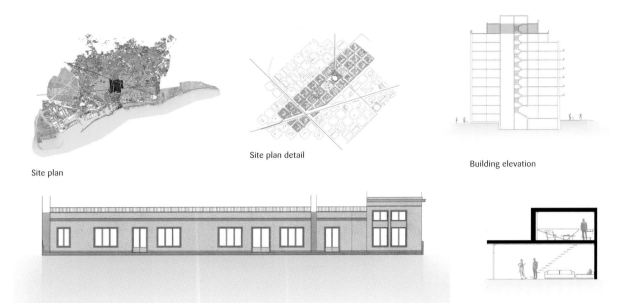

Site plan

Site plan detail

Building elevation

Facade

Section

Floor plan

In the home office, suspended lights in Lampe Gras model Acrobates in chrome, a Premier table with a metal structure and alabaster tabletop by Cattelan Italia, and Aeron chairs by Herman Miller have been chosen.

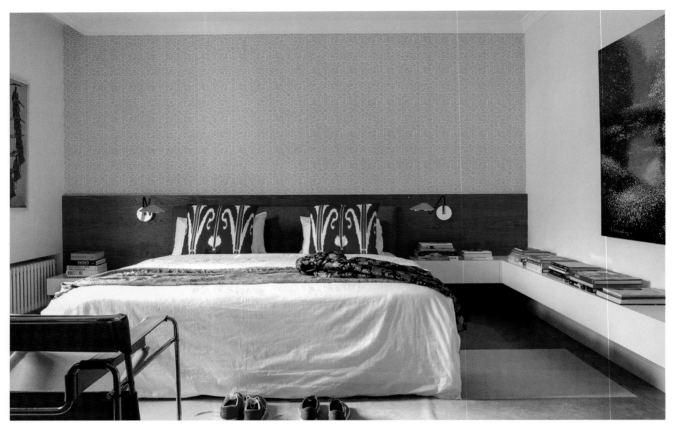

017

A bespoke headboard has been designed with suspended bedside tables that extend from one side as a shelf, contributing to a feeling of continuity and visual lightness.

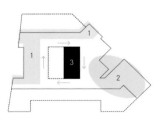

Zone layout

1. Night area   3. Service
2. Day area   4. Terrace

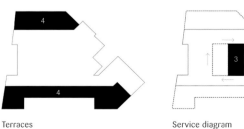

Terraces

Service diagram

SAGRADA FAMILIA

PEDESTRIAN WALKWAY. GREEN AREA

Views scheme

018

It is important to choose outdoor furniture that is suitable for weather changes. Teakwood ensures resistance to sun, air, and rain. A roll-up sail is a good option for protection during the hours of greatest solar radiation.

Park Avenue Residence

2,100 sq ft

New York City, New York,
United States

Hariri & Hariri Architecture

© Eric Laignel

The owners of this apartment on Park Avenue are a couple
whose children, now grown up, are no longer living with
them. So, they decided to look for a more compact home,
in accordance with their new way of life. The two-bedroom
apartment has been designed around a spacious loft-style living
and dining area.

White, which stands out as the absolute star, is the perfect
backdrop to display a large collection of art chosen by the
owner with the help of his son, who is an artist and art dealer.
With the display of the artwork being the main goal, the lighting
has been carefully selected, making this home a fascinating
place that exudes beauty and peace.

019

Mirrored decoration in modern homes is key to embellishing the environment and giving a unique touch to your style. It also brings light and visually expands the space.

The flooring is mostly oak, stained with a pale gray. The walls are all uninterrupted "floating walls" without light switches or base moldings and are painted in a shade of white called "Calm," ready to display bold contemporary art.

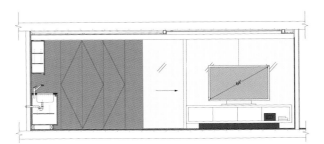

Family room. East elevation

020

The kitchen is partially open, so spatial continuity and interaction between the different spaces is not lost, but instead space is gained for a work counter and a cooking area.

Family room. North elevation

Floor plan

1. Entry hall
2. Powder room
3. Coat closet
4. Dining room
5. Living room
6. Master bedroom
7. Master closet
8. Master bathroom
9. Bathroom
10. Bedroom
11. Family room
12. Kitchen

021

The countertop is extended to create a bar for breakfast or a snack so that you don't always have to use the dining room. Although the kitchen is open, the floor and the bar delimit the space.

022

Adjustable wall-washers illuminate the paintings, whilst decorative fixtures tell a parallel story of inviting nature inside. Organically branching chandeliers from Studio Bertjan Pot were chosen for the key areas above the living room coffee table and dining table.

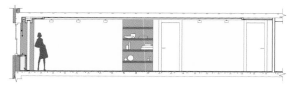

Living room. South elevation

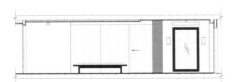

Living room. West elevation

Living room. North elevation

023

A working area has been cleverly designed along the window. This makes the most of the light coming in. The all-white furniture ensures that the feeling of spaciousness is not lost.

Shades of Play

7,000 sq ft

Chicago, Illinois, United States

Interior design: PROjECT
Architect: dSpace Studio

© Tony Soluri, Aimeé Mazzenga,
 Gianni Franchellucci

This project responds to the desire of its owners, an elegant and sophisticated couple with three children, for a new home with a modern structure that reflects their inclination towards pure lines, with a dose of color, and that is also automated.

After an impressive three-story facade covered with zinc panels, one discovers an interior as daring as its architecture, with unexpected color combinations, contrasting textures, and fun shapes. It is an interior that oozes the essence of its owners: a couple who enjoys expressing themselves through fashion, art, and design.

The folded-steel staircase connecting floors two and three is visible from the double-height living area, animated with artworks by Marlon Portales Cusett and Vladimir León Sagols.

024

To give cohesion to the whole, the palette is echoed in the second-floor library. Along one wall, custom rift-cut oak shelving with acrylic dividers frame a channel-back banquette in rosy mohair. Suspended from the ceiling, a sculpture of brass geometric shapes cascades through a cutout in the floor down into the piano gallery below.

At 7,000 square feet spread across 2.5 city lots, the architects drafted and delivered on five bedrooms, seven bathrooms, an office, a command center, a kick-ass hangout lounge for their kids, a garage top sport court, and more.

Third floor plan

Second floor plan

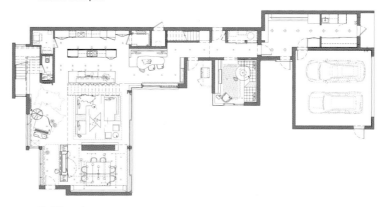

First floor plan

025

The kitchen serves as a backdrop to the formal living room. In order not to clash with the surroundings, the high-contrast marble extractor hood was revisited, which has the appearance of an abstract work of art.

The dining room can accommodate
six people on wool-upholstered Cédric
Ragot chairs and more on a mohair-
covered custom bench; above it is a
painted-fabric triptych by Gina Dorough.

026

The color palette gets softer and
more ethereal when you walk up
to the bedrooms. The more daring
colors give way to brass, silver, and
white for a quiet, intimate area.

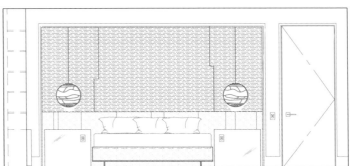

Master bedroom elevations

027

The brass panels cladding the wall next to the bath enhance the brightness of the space by reflecting the sunlight coming through the skylight.

Master bath elevations

Tribeca Penthouse Loft

1,300 sq ft

New York, New York,
United States

Studio Gild

© Mike Schwartz Photography

Artwork takes center stage in this New York City pied-à-terre.
Sleek, modern furnishings and intentional blank spaces allow
for a gallery-like experience while retaining a comfortable, laid-
back atmosphere required of a city refuge. The bold, at times
shocking, artwork acts as the focal point, while the surrounding
furnishings and accessories play the role of supporting
characters.

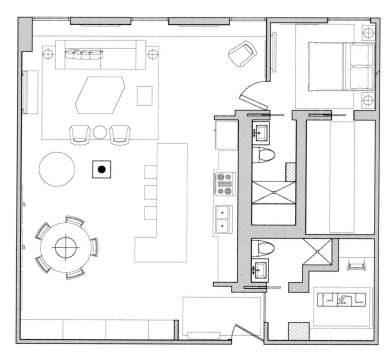

Floor plan

028

The flaxen throw color is warm and bright, yet simultaneously very cheeky and intense. Introduced in moderation and in contrast with the taupes and grays, it is elegant and sophisticated.

Leather is a versatile material that complements any space. In this restrained, sophisticated dining room, leather chairs serve as a counterpoint to disrupt the chromatic uniformity with elegant warmth.

029

Although floating furniture occupies a similar footprint to that of heavier furniture with legs, the visual sensation is much lighter and more successful for smaller spaces.

030

Replacing the headboard
with an over-scaled, dramatic
painting by Whitney Bedford
gives the bedroom a complete
transformation. Art fills the room
with life and color. It is possible
then to keep the remaining
furnishings very minimalist
without missing a detail.

Apartment in Tel Aviv

1,378 sq ft

Tel Aviv, Israel

Aviram-Kushmirski

© Oded Smadar

The owners of this apartment were looking for an exclusive design that would be a true reflection of their personality and lifestyle. A personalization of the highest quality, a "haute couture" design that would create sensations of glamour, elegance, and luxury, together, of course, with a warm, pleasant, and comfortable atmosphere that would provide the necessary functionality for a family.

The result is a clean, stylish space that stands out for its precise design and careful attention to detail. Exciting and unusual links were created between shapes, textures, objects, and art.

Floor plan

1. Living room
2. Dining room
3. Kitchen
4. Master bedroom
5. Bedroom 1
6. Bedroom 2
7. Walk-in closet

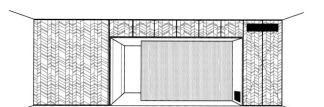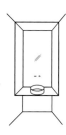

Isometric

031

An apartment with many columns and beams was transformed into a broad, open space. The elements disrupting the original space were integrated into the design concept and became an integral part of it.

032

A cleverly designed bar cabinet whose doors, when closed, are absolutely integrated into the wall was created. This creates a cleaner aesthetic sensation and helps to generate a greater sense of spaciousness.

The wealth of materials used comprises
a wide range that includes metal, wood,
and marble combined in surfaces and in
large volumes, very carefully arranged
in layers and blocks with different
finishes.

033

The black-and-white theme is synonymous with elegance and sobriety. In order not to overwhelm the space, the predominant color is white. Gold details add a touch of luxury and sophistication to the whole.

The chromatic palette—white, black, and gold notes—of materials is extended to the whole house. As in the living room, the herringbone-patterned wooden wall camouflages the dressing room doors.

034

Marble is one of the best materials for bathrooms because of its durable nature and timeless appearance. It also brings elegance, style, and sophistication, and its different veins and glints make each piece unique.

Rocabella

2,000 sq ft

Montreal, Quebec, Canada

Kelli Richards Designs

© Drew Hadley

Situated in downtown Montreal, this luxurious pied-à-terre was designed for a family with exceptional taste. The designer's work included selecting, designing, and procuring all furniture, lighting, and decor as well as designing and installing custom built-ins and bath vanities.

The dining area has a custom-built shelving unit with wood paneling mixed with lacquered and marble shelves for the client to display some of her favorite vases and accessories.

All of the furniture was selected or designed with a focus on quality, beauty, and elegance, with many pieces imported from Europe as well as some unique custom pieces designed by the Kelli Richards Designs team.

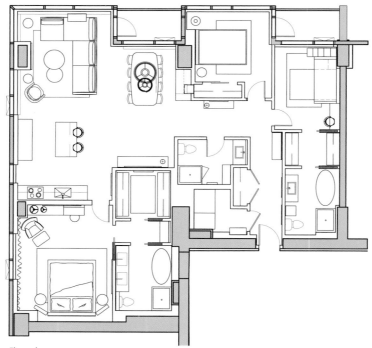

Floor plan

035

A hefty column in the living room was covered with large tiles imported from Italy. This way, what could have been an obstacle becomes a decorative element that gives peronality to the room.

036

Sometimes there are lamps whose main function, that of giving light, is as important as their decorative function. Such is the case of this original lamp that seems to float over the dining table and gives it a modern and innovative style.

Built-in shelving unit elevation

Side view

037

Bronze-tinted mirror wall panels installed in the hallway visually enlarge the space and add to the opulence of the unit.

The decoration of the bedroom is based on very soft gray and neutral tones. The chromatic harmony as well as the chosen furniture and decorative accessories transmit a sensation of tranquility that invites you to relax.

038

The main advantage of the customized cabinets is that they are completely adapted to the available dimensions as well as to the storage needs. In addition to fitting perfectly, they are unique pieces that bring personality and distinction to the home—a perfect combination of aesthetics and versatility.

Master closet built-in elevation

Master closet built-in side view

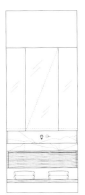

Bathroom vanity elevation

Bathroom vanity side view

Set in a former factory, this house presents a refined yet robust interior underpinned by thoughtful planning and strong material logic. The original warehouse was converted into a living space by architect Ivan Rijavec in 1989. Fiona Lynch distilled the layout by removing a selection of Rijavec's curves, giving modularity to the space while rounding corners in deference to the original design. This house works respectfully with the existing built fabric of Rijavec's converted warehouse, layering the interior with an emotive sense of tactility. Driven by authenticity, strength, and refinement, the result is a sleek yet calming sanctuary, a place that is truly the client's own.

Fitzroy House

2,700 sq ft
Melbourne, Victoria, Australia

Fiona Lynch

© Sharyn Cairns

The kitchen, now anchored by a
monumental hewn granite countertop,
is paired with a striking range hood
shrouded in oxidized brass that serves
as the focal point of the space.

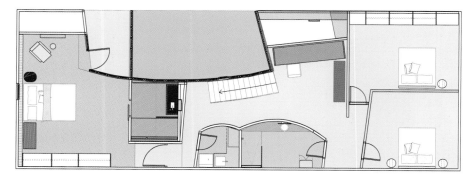

Upper floor plan

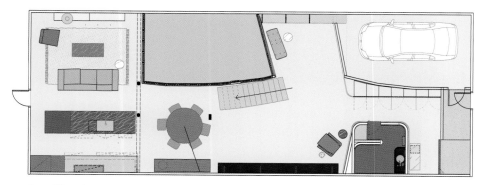

Ground floor plan

Inspired by the client's love of mountaineering and the outdoors, textured granite, polished plaster, and deep stained timber reference the earthy hues and nuanced textures found in nature.

The existing concrete floor was
bushhammered and left bare.

New windows to the atrium's living room side provide enhanced views of the refreshed courtyard, maximizing the sense of space in the well-lit study niche above.

Dark, sensuous tones give luminance to brush-worked textures and accents, creating a striking chiaroscuro effect.

The bathrooms embrace the mood
and seclusion of the house, combining
Nero Marquina stone and a mixture of
hand glazed Morrocan and Boffi matte
mosaic tiling.

Riverside Drive

2,400 sq ft

New York, New York,
United States

D'Aquino Monaco

© Peter Margonelli

In this Riverside Drive apartment, a kinetic design of sliding lacquered wall panels has been created to highlight views of the Hudson. The clients have a clear desire for a black and white palette with grays thrown in; they were ready to make a big change in their lives and in this space. The river view now brings color in the apartment, while varying textures of plaster, lacquer, and matte surfaces create depth and interest within the mostly white palette. The flexibility of the living spaces, combined with rich textures and a play between matte and polished surfaces, allows for a truly dynamic space and a fresh setting for contemporary art and furniture.

042

The white interiors allow the focus to be put on the lines and the volumes, and also play with the light and the projected shadows, enhanced by the use of this color.

Floor plan

1. Entry
2. Powder room
3. Living &
   dining room
4. Study
5. Hall
6. Kitchen
7. Bedroom
8. Bathroom
9. Master bedroom
10. Dressing room
11. Master bathroom
12. Public hallway

A central corridor was removed to allow
the living areas to flow into one another
while drawing the light and views
further into the home.

043

The various changes in roof level and the carved polylaminate sliding doors serve to define the different spaces.

044

Thanks to the ingenuity of the designer, the column, far from being an obstacle, has been perfectly integrated into the kitchen furniture, becoming a decorative element that gives it personality.

045

When designing a custom wardrobe it is a good idea to place bars at different heights depending on the garments to be hung.

This apartment is located in the penthouse of a typical Haussmann building in Paris's 2nd district, next to the Place de la Victoire. In the past this space was occupied by three rooms originally reserved for the service. The owner, who lives abroad, wanted a pied-à-terre for himself and his family.

Overcoming the difficulty that the two structural walls posed for the distribution, he managed to design a comfortable three-room apartment whose attic ceilings give it personality and charm.

Etienne Marcel

550 sq ft
Paris, France

Peggy Bels
© Camilo Villegas

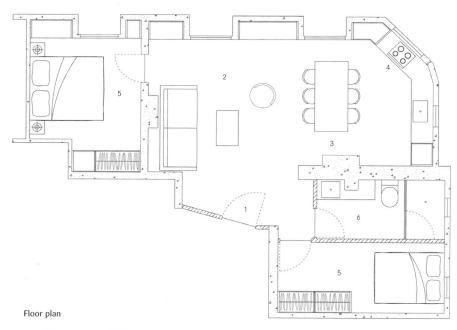

Floor plan

1. Entrance
2. Living area
3. Dining area
4. Kitchen
5. Bedroom
6. Bathroom

046

To provide warmth, a parquet floor with a herringbone arrangement, typical of Paris, has been chosen, which brings slenderness and personality to the space.

047

In this apartment of limited
dimensions the shelves embedded
in the wall are a successful
solution: they are decorative,
due to their light design they do
not detract from the feeling of
spaciousness, and they also adapt
perfectly to the attic walls.

048

The hanging lamps—besides being decorative and giving a focused light, ideal for reading—are a great choice when the room is narrow and there is not much space at the sides of the bed.

049

A good alternative to frame the bed without a headboard is to paint that wall a different color than the rest of the walls. The headboard wall is the one that should stand out, so it will have a more striking color, but this should always be looking for harmony with the whole, as well.

Grand Street Residence

3,000 sq ft

New York, New York,
United States

**Alexander Butler | Design
Services, LLC (AB|DS)**

© Andrii Zhulidov

This project was conceived of as a case study in the Soho neighborhood dichotomies: grit and polish, old and new, traditional character and modern detailing. AB|DS retained those classic and familiar features such as exposed brick walls, decorative tin ceilings, and concrete flooring which serves as the framework, but then seamlessly slipped a contemporary and elegant—but also inviting—home within. One is particularly struck by the level of artisanship in this project—construction perfection may be hard to achieve, but this is close. Additionally, the refined materials, such as polished marble, pristine glass, and quartered oak, nest effortlessly with the gritty brick, cast-iron columns, and articulated tin: a little slice of Soho right inside.

050

The kitchen features a palette of oak wood veneers, Carrara marble, and gunmetal reveals. AB|DS employed pocket-and-pivot door systems, stone-front drawers, and glass display for maximum alignment of aesthetics and function.

Kitchen elevation

051

Almost as important as the design and function of the kitchen cabinetry is that of the lighting. Thoughtful consideration is given to the layouts in order to create the most effective zones for both mood and task lighting. Recessed lights for general illumination, puck lighting for cooking tasks, and strip lighting to highlight the beautiful stonework were all employed, as well as a custom decorative chandelier for a bistro-like atmosphere.

Black and white is a concept used extensively in the project, from the gunmetal wrapped doors found within bright, airy spaces like the mudroom, to the literal veining and coloration of the powder room Nero Marquina Stone, to the artwork itself.

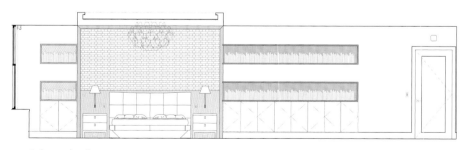

Bedroom elevation

052

In the master bedroom, the brick wall is framed with a custom, clean-lined wood armature and all of its imperfections are highlighted with accent lighting recessed into the headbooard. Tin ceiling panels were reclaimed from the original apartment and reinstalled with modern embellishments, as well.

053

In this master bathroom, the clients
wanted an open concept room,
while still maintaining normal
divisions of space and privacy.
Hers-and-His custom vanities float
from ¾ height marble dividing
walls, which separate the bath and
shower room, while a continuous
floating ceiling above and dark
graphite tile below (in cleft finish
for grip) unify the two spaces.

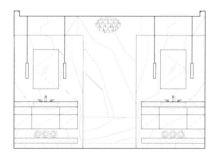

Bathroom elevation

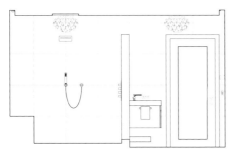

Bathroom elevation

Balmes

2,368 sq ft

Terrassa, Spain

Abrils Studio

© Abrils Studio

The clients were looking for a plot of land or a newly built house to start their new adventure, a family. Fortunately, they did not have to wait long to find an empty lot in the center of town where they could build their dream house—a two-story house in a linear and very architectural style, with large windows on both facades, which flood the space with light, and a large garden. The predominance of white, splashed with colorful brushstrokes, complemented by the natural wood that covers the floor, makes this an elegant and warm home that transmits peace in the middle of the urban environment in which it is located.

On the ground floor there is a garage for two cars, the entrance, a courtesy toilet, and the day area—kitchen, dining room, and living room—which is open to a large garden. The upper floor has three bedrooms, two bathrooms, a study, and a laundry area.

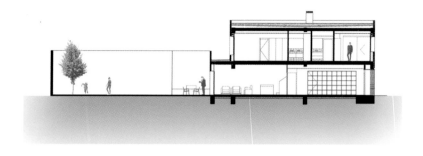

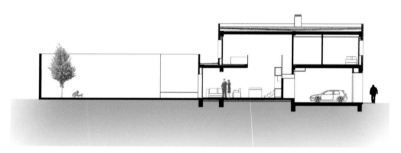

Sections

Second floor plan

First floor plan

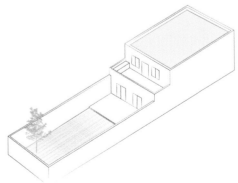

Axonometric view

054

Overlapping carpets have become a trend. They allow you to cover large spaces with standard carpets without having to order them to measure, and they bring a lot of personality to a room thanks to the particular play of volumes, textures, and colors.

055

By painting the kitchen cabinets white they are fully integrated into the space, maintaining the feeling of spaciousness and spatial continuity.

056

The floor slab that was just above the kitchen island has been removed to create a double space that allows the visual connection of the two floors and light to flow into every corner of the house.

057

The studio, with capacity for two people, has been strategically located in front of the terrace and opens to the double space, which ensures a great entry of natural light, something that is very important for work performance.

058

The windows of the entire house have been dressed with linen curtains that allow them to sieve the sunlight during the hours of maximum exposure without losing clarity. Linen is also a natural, light, elegant, and very fresh fabric.

Brentwood

10,000 + 2,000 sq ft

Los Angeles, California,
United States

**Interior design: Meg
Joannides, MLK Studio
Architect: Belzberg Architects**

© Art Gray Photography

This project consisted of creating a complete interior design
scheme for a modern 10,000 sq ft main residence as well as
a 2,000 sq ft guest house. In addition to the interiors, Meg
Joannides of MLK Studio was hired to design the ten bathrooms
as well as the main kitchen and the kitchen of the guest house in
collaboration with Boffi. A great part of the furniture was designed
by the studio and manufactured in trusted local workshops in
Los Angeles. A neutral color palette predominates throughout
the house, and textures have been skilfully blended to create
the depth and layers that are visible in the sophisticated design.

059

In addition to their decorative function, wooden shelves serve to create interesting plays of light and shadow that change throughout the day, adding dynamism to the space.

060

All materials were thoughtfully
selected to harmonize with the
architect's vision for the building.
Walnut hardwood flooring
throughout as well as bluestone
countertops coordinate with the
architect's stacked bluestone walls.

061

Less is more. Order, symmetry, and simplicity of form dominate in this room where a single work of art is enough to break that uniformity and bring the space to life.

First floor plan

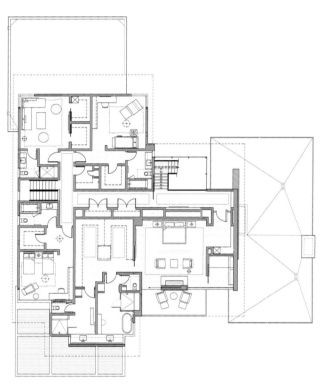

Second floor plan

062

The backlit mirrors provide ambient light when the general light is not wanted on; also, by not needing an extra wall light to illuminate the wash area, they allow for cleaner walls, perfect in contemporary and minimalist style bathrooms.

The kitchen worktop in Calacatta marble and the glossy white cabinets respond to the customer's express wish for a neutral palette.

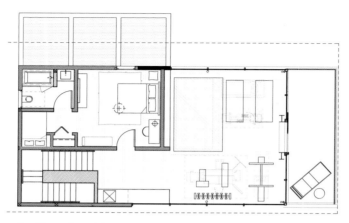

Guest house. Second floor

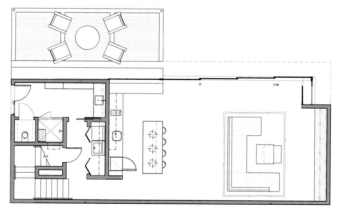

Guest house. First floor

The black-and-white theme runs throughout the guest house, bringing uniformity to the decoration. The palette of neutral tones is complemented by the use of wood to provide a note of warmth and elegance.

When the windows are opened, the limits between the interior and exterior disappear and the spaces are integrated as a whole. The porch and the garden become extensions of the house itself, so it is important that there is absolute harmony in the design of the different spaces.

This new housing concept maximizes usability and takes advantage of the performance of ALVIC equipment by creating a type of use that is constructive, completely free of stereotypes and decorative conventions.

A project where movement flows and where a new concept of intelligent habitability is generated.The material unites, breaks from one plane to another faithful to the route and the creative design that the architect has imagined, thus allowing to connect rooms that need very diverse functions and utilities.

The success of this project is the breadth in function and perspective of a very small meter plan, a modern and updated version of living-lounging.

ALVIC Smart Home

301 sq ft
Madrid, Spain

**Ruiz Velázquez
architecture & design**

© Nacho Uribe Salazar

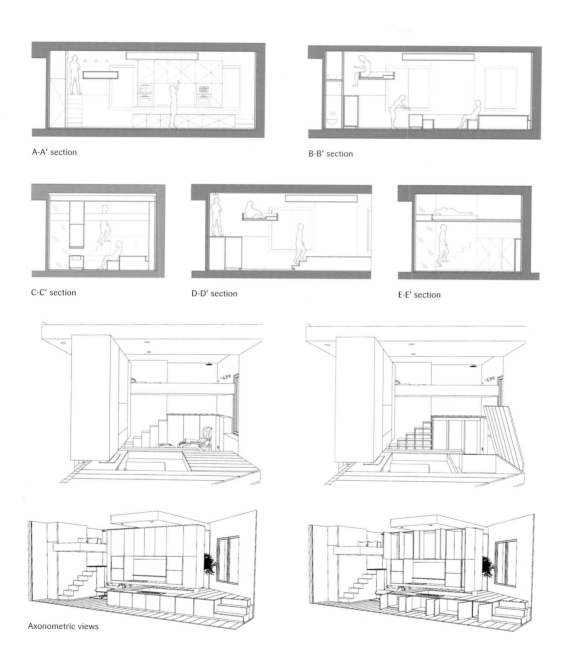

A-A' section

B-B' section

C-C' section

D-D' section

E-E' section

Axonometric views

The project structures the space from the three-dimensionality, in width, length, and especially height, one of the least used coordinates in the design of homes. The challenge is visible in the few available meters of the project's floor plan, where it is possible to hide, store, and show in all dimensions the uses and functions that are essential for daily life.

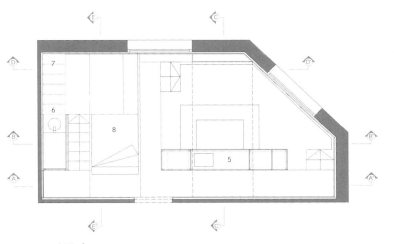

2,10 A.F.F. plan

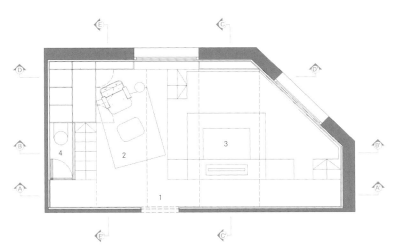

Floor plan

1. Entry
2. Living room
3. Lounge
4. Toilet
5. Kitchen
6. Bathroom
7. Shower
8. Bedroom

065

The LED lights, in addition to emphasizing the silhouette and design of the furniture, are very practical when creating more intimate and relaxed environments in the living room—ideal for relaxing on the sofa watching TV with soft lighting.

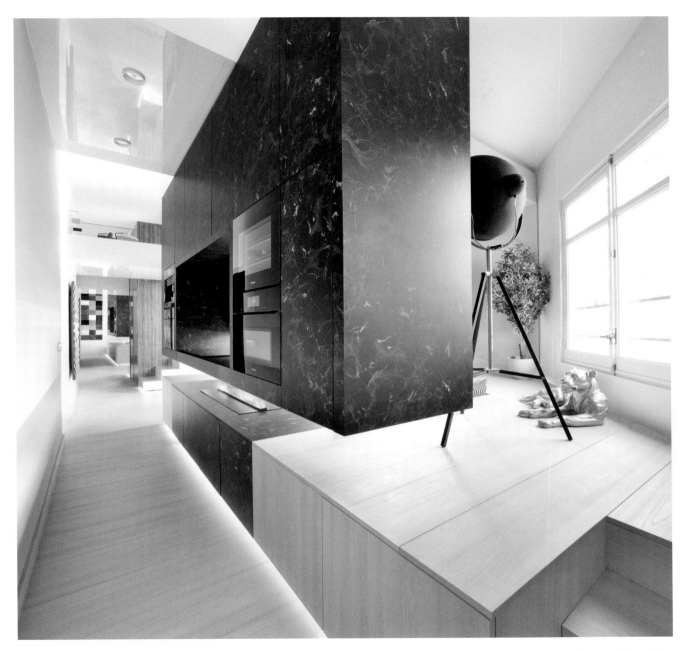

The objective of the design is a space that has no limits, to escape from the classic horizontal compartmentalization of the rooms, to treat the project as a three-dimensional object, where each point of the residence can be located by specifying the axes of coordinates.

The central black volume on one side houses the functions of the kitchen, and on the other it has the TV, which can be hidden when not in use. As it is suspended, it divides the space without losing the sensation of spatial continuity.

The different surfaces are covered with panels manufactured with the latest technology that provides the design, through a synchronized finish, with all the beauty and realism of natural wood.

068

Constructively, it is a sustainable design, a model of constructive eco-design, systematized and articulated in an intelligent way according to the needs of our times—a space built in a modular and completely adaptable way that can perfectly change its scale and forms.

High Times

10,000 sq ft

Chicago, Illinois, United States

Interior Design: PROjECT
Architect: Filoramo Talsma
Architecture

© Cynthia Lynn Kim

Located at the top of one of the most luxurious addresses on the Mag Mile, this elegant duplex penthouse is a member of the "Mile High Club" of Chicago residences. This is a collaborative project between the architect and the interior designer, whose teamwork has resulted in a true sanctuary in the Gold Coast neighborhood for a family of five. Starting with three units, a single apartment was designed, where there is a continuous flow between its functional spaces and where a number of new ones have been added, such as a room to receive visitors and a yoga and meditation studio. All of this is decorated in an avant-garde style that impregnates it with an air of elegant exclusivity.

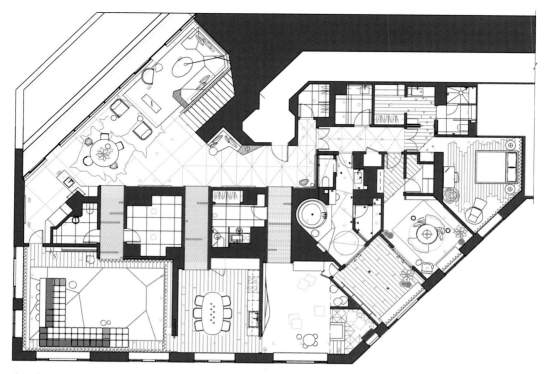

Floor plan

The penthouse houses four bedrooms including a large master suite, a professional-level chef's kitchen with a breakfast nook, and a formal dining room. In addition to this, there is a lounge area, a bar, a yoga and meditation area, a children's playroom, and an adjacent guest suite with a spa-like bathroom for out-of-towners.

069

The Kenyan marble in the bar denotes elegance and exclusivity. The arrangement of the white veins composes a surface that is simply spectacular and that changes according to the entrance of light.

A sinuous, three-dimensional sculpture
by Chicago artist Eric Gushee becomes
the focal point of the living room.

070

Mixing chairs of different styles around a table is a new trend. It may seem risky; however, as long as the mix is harmonious, it will add a cool, personal touch to the decor.

One of the best ways to bring the walls of a home to life is to hang original paintings that add notes of color. If these works are also jewels like these signed by Andy Warhol, the result is unique.

071

Total white is a good option for decorating the corridors as it enlarges and illuminates these areas that are generally lacking in natural light.

072

Lighting plays a fundamental role in creating an intimate and cozy atmosphere, like the one achieved by this original lamp made of bicycle chains that gives off a soft and warm light.

Contemporary Twilight

5,480 sq ft

Aventura, Florida, United States

DKOR Interiors

© Alexia Fodere

The residence was designed for a Mexican family who recently moved to Florida to pursue a better environment to raise their children.

The inspiration behind this dream home was the essence of twilight—that moment at the end of the day when all the hustle of the day has come to a peaceful close, and the family can find tranquility in their home as the sun sets, revealing the beautiful blue and amber tones of twilight.

The interior design details and features remain cohesive throughout the entire home, based on vertical movement and hues.

Particular material selections, like variations in wood, concrete, and subtle stone patterns, create a unique mood for this elegant and functional home.

The accent colors used throughout the home—namely, shades of blue and gray, with pops of amber—are inspired by the essence of a twilight sky.

073

Glass railings are the best option for modern spaces, where you want to give a sense of spaciousness and light. Despite being less common, not only do they provide extraordinary safety as there are no gaps between their panels, but they are also an incredible decorative element in themselves.

074

When the bedroom is very large, a part can be reserved for the installation of a living or working area. It is ideal to place it next to the window to make the most of the entry of natural light.

075

The same chromatic scheme, as
well as the palette of materials,
is also extended in the bedrooms
where, on a neutral base, blue and
amber details are added to walls,
furniture, and fabrics to give life
and personality to each one of
the rooms.

076

If the space allows it, it is a good option to have a complete water area: a shower for the day-to-day, where we go with more haste, and a bathtub reserved for moments of relaxation.

High Line

2,140 sq ft
New York, New York,
United States

B Interior

© Federica Carlet

This elegant apartment is perfectly situated in the heart of West Chelsea, overlooking the lush gardens of the Manhattan High Line.

B Interior created a minimalist interior design that complements the building's modern architecture. The furnishings accentuate the floor-to-ceiling windows and the high ceilings. Clean lines and carefully selected accents draw attention without distracting from the architectural features of the space.

Custom wood panels in the living room and master bedroom act as a functional element (TV surround and shelf above the bed) as well as an enriching accent.

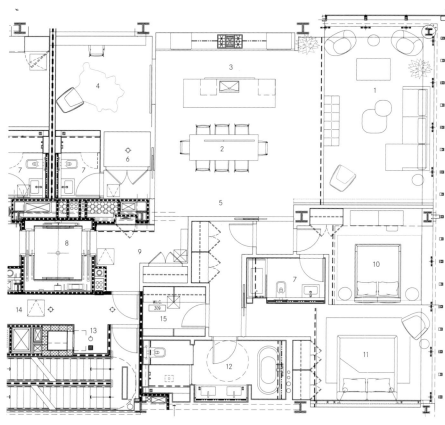

Floor plan

1. Living room
2. Dining room
3. Kitchen
4. Study
5. Corridor
6. Laundry
7. Bathroom
8. Elevator
9. Foyer
10. Bedroom
11. Master bedroom
12. Master bathroom
13. Trash chute
14. Exit corridor
15. Walk-in closet

The designer has the uncanny ability to bridge a modern, sophisticated aesthetic with a functional and inviting living space.

077

With a composition reminiscent of a Mondrian painting, a module has been designed to house the television, and creates a large storage area as well.

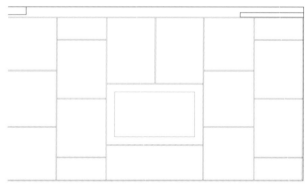

Sketch

078

The kitchen island, with an elegant simplicity in its design, in addition to being a work area, is a storage area that also serves as a space divider.

The two bedrooms follow a similar color scheme. On a base of gray tones, the cushions and bedding add a note of color and the front wall adds texture and personality to the design.

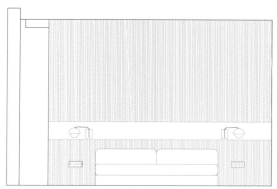

Headboard sketch

Sunset Harbour I

2,196 sq ft

Miami Beach, Florida,
United States

Studio RODA

© Claudia Uribe

The owners of this modern residence came to Studio RODA with a very specific request: to design a serene, oasis-like environment with an additional third bedroom. To meet the request without obstructing the apartment's natural light, the studio employed a muted palette of earthen hues and tactile materials, ranging from smooth monochrome granite countertops and subtle gold-lined fixtures to buttery leather furnishings and sheer, sunlight-diffusing curtains. Privacy without additional weight was achieved through floating space dividers, while select custom furnishings inject more character into the home.

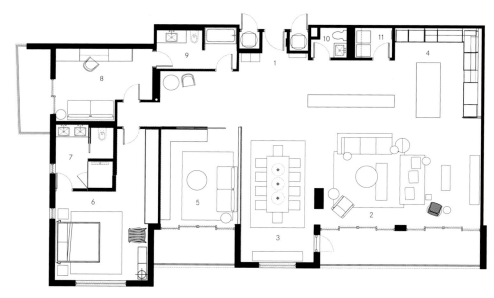

1. Foyer
2. Living room
3. Dining room
4. Kitchen
5. Library/guest bedroom
6. Master bedroom
7. Master bathroom
8. Office
9. Guest bathroom
10. Powder room
11. Laundry

Floor plan

079

Next to the sofa, a huge stool serves as a seat for the two areas, the living room and the TV area, while dividing both rooms.

080

Putting two nesting tables as a coffee table, apart from its aesthetic interest, has the advantage that its size can be varied according to the room's needs, since one fits inside the other and, moreover, if needed, they can also be used separately.

The library, which is open to the
distributor, can be converted into a guest
room. For this reason it has a sliding
door that allows the privacy of this
space to be preserved when necessary.

The mirrored backsplash provides depth and luminosity to the elegant kitchen area.

081

The wooden module behind the sofa delimits the living area and houses a bar and storage area.

082

As if it were a painting, the view that is framed in the window next to the bed adds a note of color and fills with life the bedroom in which the predominance of white is absolute.

Although with different patterns and materials, the two bathrooms share the same chromatic base: white walls with black details and a white washbasin under a black top.

Brazil Design

3,573 sq ft
São Paulo, Brazil

Diego Revollo Arquitetura

© Alain Brugier

At the client's request, the design of this apartment was to be masculine, sophisticated, and timeless. Additionally, the layout had to guarantee spatial integration and fluidity. The layout, designed to welcome and reinforce coexistence, stands out for the sequence of warm and interconnected environments; there are no small, isolated spaces but rather harmonious spaces with multiple functions that can be used according to the occasion.

Diego Revollo creates a unique project, where a Brazilian design stands out as a great protagonist—the colors, the details, and the arrangement of the furniture guarantee an original and, at the same time, cosmopolitan result.

083

To give the space personality, and to accentuate the masculine character of the project, a set of sliding and pivoting doors covers the entire perimeter of the entrance vestibule, forming a black, sophisticated, and slightly industrial volume that contrasts the gray shades of the rest of the structure.

After the refurbishment the living room
is completely open to the terrace area,
where the dining room and kitchen
are located, so the three rooms are
connected.

Before floor plan

After floor plan

084

Mineral Portland porcelain tiles
from Portobello Shop Gabriel
cover the floor of both the living
room and the terrace, so the two
areas are completely integrated.

In the dining room, the Milla table and Clad chairs are by Brazilian designer Jader Almeida.

085

The use of different materials creates interesting contrasts of textures without breaking with the chromatic palette, which ranges from white to black through a wide range of grays. The polished travertine marble contrasts with the matte black of the cabinets and becomes a focal point in the space.

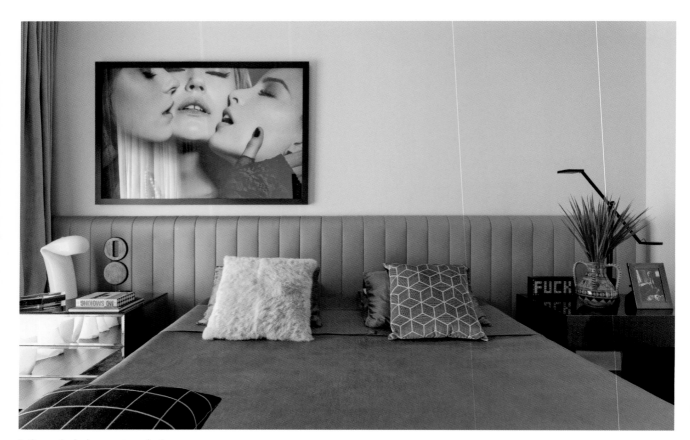

In the master bedroom, a taupe leather
headboard from the Brazilian firm
Quartos Etc. adds a touch of color to
the ensemble.

086

To decorate the courtesy toilet in a striking, sophisticated, or original way, wallpaper is a very good option, like this one from the firm Celina Dias. Normally used as a guest bathroom, the courtesy toilet does not have a shower, which allows this decorative resource to be used without fear of being peeled off by hot water vapor.

A Modernist Take
on a Classic Cottage

4,500 sq ft

San Francisco, California,
United States

John Lum Architecture

© Paul Dyer

Charming cottage style in the front; cool multilevel modern in
the back. John Lum Architecture renovated this residence to
maximize views while preserving the neighborhood's architectural
integrity. An engineering masterpiece, the house was rebuilt
from its foundation and encompasses a four-bed, four-bath
main house and a separate one-bed, one-bath garden unit.

Keeping with the area's vernacular, the front facade was
retained (but reinterpreted) while an uncompromising modern
addition was added in the rear. Floor-to-ceiling windows and
the exposed steel frame the downtown skyline and create an
unusual high-rise sensibility.

Front elevation

Rear elevation

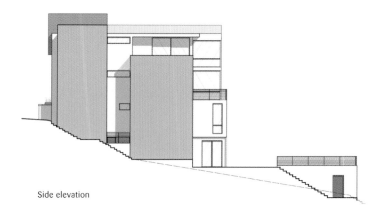

Side elevation

Multiple roof terraces reflect California's quintessential indoor-outdoor lifestyle. A private backyard, which sits atop the two-car garage, is the perfect play space.

Basement plan

First floor plan

Second floor plan

Third floor plan

The basement houses a separate
dwelling with an open floor plan
consisting of living and dining areas,
a kitchen, bedroom with en-suite bath,
and a garden space.

087

In this house, the staircase is no longer just another construction element but a decorative one. As it is open, it gives a sensation of greater brightness and allows light to pass through it, creating interesting plays of light and shadows.

The large open kitchen, coupled with the various seating areas, including a play section, makes this an ideal home to receive visitors.

088

The kitchen appliances have been paneled in the same wood as the cabinets and island to create a uniform whole. In this way, the kitchen area is clearly differentiated from the rest of the living area without the need for any additional separators.

The oval tub, tucked into the glass corner of the master bath, provides a romantic perch with exceptional city views.

Clear Water Bay

1,800 sq ft

Hong Kong, China

Peggy Bels

© Geoffroy Renard

This apartment is located in an unbeatable environment. Surrounded by a lush park, its large windows allow you to enjoy spectacular views. However, although it was new, its owners wanted to change its distribution to adapt it to their needs. As a result, an elegant and contemporary apartment with simple and pure lines was obtained. With cement walls, metal details, and a neutral color palette with small color accents, it incorporates elements that make reference to the origins of its owners, Canada and Hong Kong, as well as Japan, where they lived together for a long time.

089

The living room features floor-to-ceiling windows that fully open to draw the surrounding greenery into the living space.

The rooftop terrace, which is the same size as the apartment, has a spacious living area and a dining area with a barbecue where you can enjoy pleasant leisure time surrounded by nature.

090

The kitchen, originally separated at the back of the floor, was moved to the front and opened to the living room, allowing for social interaction. The mixture of materials manages to create interesting contrasts of textures that enrich the space.

091

The bedding plays as important a role as the furniture or the color of the wall in the decoration of a bedroom. Here we have chosen a blanket and cushions of a pink tone that bring warmth to the room and are an invitation to rest.

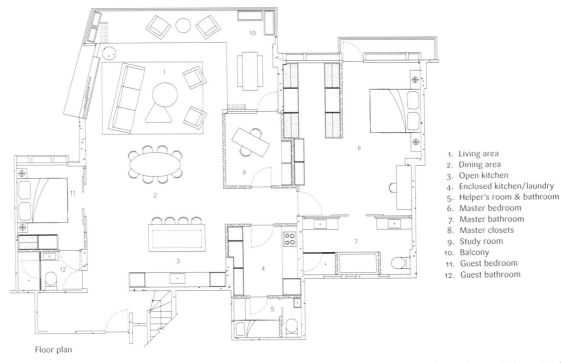

Floor plan

1. Living area
2. Dining area
3. Open kitchen
4. Enclosed kitchen/laundry
5. Helper's room & bathroom
6. Master bedroom
7. Master bathroom
8. Master closets
9. Study room
10. Balcony
11. Guest bedroom
12. Guest bathroom

In the new layout, the four original bedrooms were turned into a large master bedroom with a dressing room and bathroom, a guest room with an en-suite bathroom, and an office. The living area was also extended and is now connected to the kitchen and the dining room.

The materials, the sobriety, and the composition of this spectacular bathroom with a spa soul are clearly inspired by Japan.

Picture Perfect

5,300 sq ft

Chicago, Illinois, United States

PROjECT

© Cynthia Lynn Kim

The owners of this house had bought it with the idea that it would become a forever home. They loved its location, its layout, and its generosity of space. However, they wanted to change the finishes, fleeing from the standard houses, to give it a custom-made contemporary air. After making the necessary structural changes—such as removing moldings and baseboards—and replacing faucets, hardware, bathroom countertops, and lighting fixtures with more modern ones, they gave free rein to the decoration, resulting in a home of pure lines with a curiously chic decor and an undeniable personality.

In the living room, highlights include Hannah Vaughan's Post Industrial Reservoir Floor Lamp from Pavilion Antiques & 20th C and a pair of crisp white leather Barcelona chairs.

A two-sided fireplace separates the living room from the dining room and allows both spaces to benefit from its warmth.

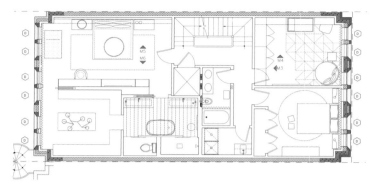

Third floor plan

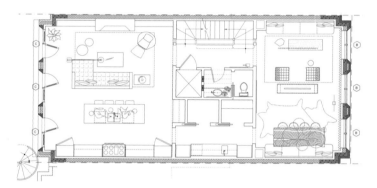

Second floor plan

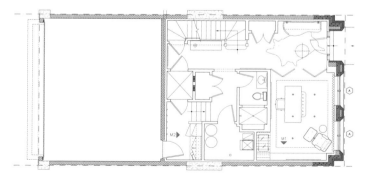

First floor plan

The walnut stools by IONDesign
serve as a counterpoint to the gray
that predominates in the kitchen and,
together with the Flos Aim hanging
lamps, add personality to the whole.

092

The home's traditional staircase was upgraded from conventional oak handrails, balustrades, and stringers to sleek, hand-wrought blackened steel, which has totally changed the feel of the entire house.

Clearance 6'-4"

Proceed to yellow panel

Slow. Drive with caution.

Proceed to yellow panel

Stop at yellow panel

093

Carpets decorate the space as well as protect the floor from footprints and our feet from the cold. They also help to create a cozy and comfortable atmosphere.

Jewel Box

430 sq ft
New York, New York,
United States

Messana O'Rorke

© Eric Laignel

The clients, a couple with no children, wanted a pied-à-terre evoking a room at a boutique hotel, albeit with a hidden bedroom and ample space to accommodate cooking and entertaining. In its original state, this was a typical studio apartment, with a bed in the living area, a galley kitchen, a bathroom with a tub, and two built-in closets.

The goal was to maximize the physical and atmospheric size of the apartment by designing multiple spaces that fit efficiently into an organized structure, creating the illusion of a larger space. The architects found inspiration in everyday objects that are simultaneously beautiful and efficient: jewelry boxes, steamer trunks, and even RVs.

094

The bed "container," clad in unlacquered brass, was inserted into the space three feet from the entry door and three feet from the northern storage unit, achieving the client mandate of a hidden bedroom while also creating an entry vestibule and a hallway.

095

Custom-designed European fumed oak-faced storage was installed along the north and south walls, acting as a layer of soundproofing between apartments. The northern storage unit contains books, clothing, and a television.

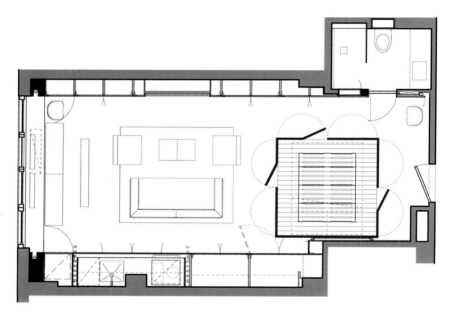

Floor plan

096

The living area now functions as just that, with a custom oak table spanning the length of the window and acting as both a "front porch" (overlooking the city and offering amazing sunset views) and a desk that can be reconfigured as a dining table when entertaining guests.

097

The inside of this gleaming
structure is lined in gray Italian
cowhide. The base of the bed is
raised, creating additional storage
underneath, allowing the clients to
take in the aforementioned views
from bed.

The reimagined bathroom, now sans tub, is completely covered in Carrara marble.

Pacific Rim

2,200 sq ft

Vancouver, British Columbia,
Canada

Robert Bailey Interiors

© Ema Peter

This downtown Vancouver pied-à-terre is needed to function as both a home away from home and an elevated entertaining space for a busy traveling couple. To translate a refined level of European design into a blank canvas, one full wall was lined in a single piece of custom-designed millwork—a showstopper with antique brass cabinet doors and a charcoal cerused oak top. There are two conversation areas, anchored with custom rugs to amplify the homeowners' opportunities to gather over fine wine.

It's a chic and inviting cosmopolitan space that works for quiet contemplation as well as it does for a pre-supper cocktail party.

098

Carpets are a valuable decorative element: they help to define spaces, give a sensation of warmth, work as thermal insulators, and absorb noise, all the while bringing personality and comfort to spaces.

Floor plan

099

Rounded shapes in decoration are important because they help to soften, balance, and even expand spaces. In addition, curves have a feminine character full of sophistication.

Design-forward furnishings—many
being new classics—are delightfully
plush and inviting and complement the
understated artwork and accessories.

Di Lido

2,637 sq ft

Miami Beach, Florida,
United States

Studio RODA

© Brian McDougall

Asked to convert this over-bright spec house into an inviting
modern home, Studio RODA drew upon its signature use of
tactile materials. A cut-stone entry wall combines with soft
white walls and sheer curtains to diffuse Florida's vivid sunlight,
while the walnut employed throughout adds dimension. Custom
furnishings supplement the subtly sophisticated residence—
from the library to the master bedroom to the dining table,
which is situated under an array of glass pendants that
showcases both the studio's nuanced approach to lighting
and its attention to even the finest details.

100

Next to the sofa there is an
ingenious piece of furniture that
serves as a sofa arm, support
table, and bookcase.

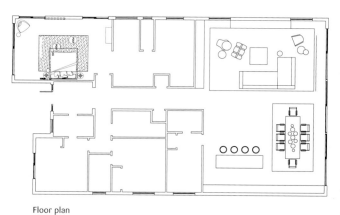

Floor plan

101

If you want to give the kitchen a
special touch, focus on the details.
The faucet features a sleek design
that makes it stand out from the
rest of the elements.

102

Despite their obvious differences, marble and wood form a perfectly balanced tandem. They complement each other, creating a wonderful fusion that, in combination with a sober and elegant design, obtains an unbeatable result.

103

In addition to providing a useful space to put objects, the niche on the wall being illuminated eliminates the need for an additional lamp on the ceiling.

This three-level home is designed to subtly "float" over the surrounding mountain environment. Given its prominent position, the motivation behind the house's design was to create a residence that could blend in with its surroundings while maximizing the views. The three-story structure, which takes the form of a three-bladed propeller, is wrapped in glass, allowing for spectacular and infinite views. Inside, an imposing glass staircase serves as the articulating axis of a modern and functional space that is also very welcoming and ideal for enjoying with family and friends.

Orum Residence

18,804 sq ft

Bel Air, Los Angeles, California, United States

SPF:architects

© Matthew Momberger

The glass curtain wall wrapping the third floor of the home is a highly sophisticated system. The structure utilizes five different widths of four different opacities—reflective, opaque, translucent, and clear—which, as an ensemble, give the structure an infinite, visually shifting, shimmering facade.

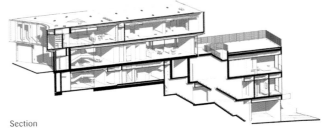

Section

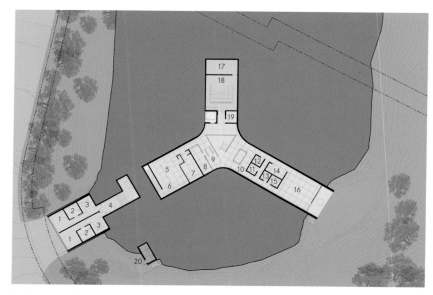

First basement plan

1. Guest room
2. Bathroom
3. Closet
4. Entry hall
5. Kitchen
6. Pantry
7. Laundry
8. Wine room
9. Wine tasting
10. Game room
11. Shower
12. Powder
13. Steam
14. Massage
15. Sauna
16. Gym
17. Mechanical room
18. Media room
19. Elevator
20. Cabana

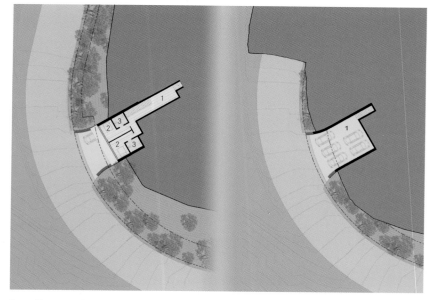

Second basement plan

Third basement plan

1. Entry hall
2. Staff room
3. Staff bathroom
4. Garage

Second level plan

1. Master suite
2. Master bathroom
3. Master closet
4. Deck
5. Den
6. Office
7. Guest suite
8. Closet
9. Bathroom
10. Mini master
11. Kitchenette
12. Linen
13. Setback line
14. Property line

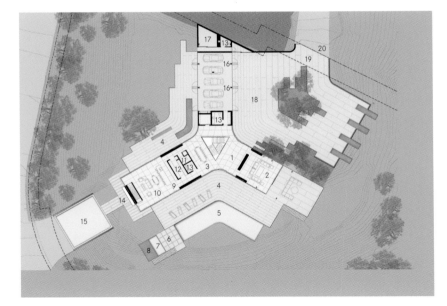

First level plan

1. Entry
2. Living room
3. Dining
4. Deck
5. Pool
6. Pavers over Baja shelf
7. Hot tub
8. Planter
9. Kitchen
10. Breakfast
11. Pantry
12. Butler's pantry
13. Powder
14. Outdoor barbecue
15. Reflection pool
16. Garage
17. Storage
18. Carport
19. Setback line
20. Property line

The program is distributed across three "blades" that radiate from a central node. The outcome of the confluence—a dynamic glass and steel staircase stretching through the core of the structure—was twofold: firstly, it provided a very straightforward answer to the vast home's circulation; secondly, it brought together what would otherwise appear as disparate areas in one's line of sight.

104

The glass walls provide a visual connection both vertically and horizontally. This makes it easy for spaces to flow into each other.

105

The marble walls are seamlessly integrated into luxurious interiors with a minimalist design, where they draw attention, acting as canvases.

106

The subtle lighting on the corridor floor generates an elegant, motivating, and attractive atmosphere while creating an interesting play of light and shadows on the walls that enhances their texture.

The walls covered with wooden slats and the comfortable sofas on which you can sit or lie down make this home cinema a dream place to enjoy long sessions of good films with friends or family.

107

The upper southwest and southeast wings of the residence house the master and mini master suites, both with 270-degree views of the city and ocean. Thanks to its barely profiled windows, the boundaries between the interior and exterior are completely blurred.

This apartment is in fact a combination of four apartments located in a former hotel turned condominiums. The clients, an international family with two children, came to New York because of their interest in the city and the art world. They are attracted to artwork that has a challenging point of view and serves as a cultural commentary—street art, among others. They have a great sense of humor in what they collect, not restricted to art, but also in their approach to living, their wardrobes, and their homes. The designer wanted to look at the apartment in an inventive way and was asked to avoid typical "luxury materials." The result is a contemporary and sculptural space, far from routine.

Central Park South

5,400 sq ft

New York, New York, United States

D'Aquino Monaco

© Stephen Kent Johnson

108

The structural column in the middle of the entrance, sheated in polished stainless steal, instead of being an obstacle, becomes the main decorative element. It also gives the space a greater visual range and creates a suggestive play of light.

Using unconventional materials and custom finishes, a faceted space that allows their collections and personalities to thrive was created.

109

Who said that swings are only for kids? This swing becomes an ideal place to read by the window or even take a relaxed nap because of its gentle sway.

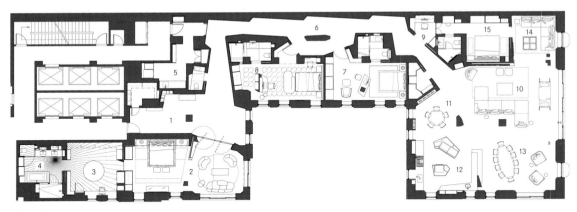

Floor plan

1. Entry
2. Master bedroom
3. Master closet
4. Master bathroom
5. Laundry
6. Hall
7. Bedroom
8. Bedroom
9. Home office
10. Living room
11. Breakfast area
12. Kitchen
13. Dining area
14. Sitting room
15. Study

Behind two impressive doors hides the main suite—composed of a cozy living room, a bedroom, a large dressing room, and a spectacular bathroom—which is at the entrance of the house, separated from the rest and offering more privacy.

110

This original module houses a storage area as well as part of the kitchen appliances that are perfectly camouflaged under the appearance of a cartoon.

This bathroom breathes luxury. The pigmented resin inlaid with gold leaf used for the sinks and bathtub turns them into real jewels, which in combination with the lighting and the mirrors form a striking ensemble that leaves no one indifferent to its charm.

Bermondsey Wall
Duplex Penthouse

2,583 sq ft

London, United Kingdom

FORMstudio

© Bruce Hemming

This penthouse has been dramatically reconfigured, creating an impressively spacious open-plan living and dining space on the upper floor. The radical design approach cleverly rationalizes the available space, celebrating the spectacular views over the Thames. From the entrance, a slot view to the river draws the visitor into a double-height space, from which elegantly detailed stairs lead up to the living area.

The penthouse is arranged over the top two floors of a prominent residential development. The original layout divided both levels into a labyrinth of cellular spaces, ignoring the spatial potential offered by the distinctive, soaring wing roof and wraparound views.

111

In addition to its main function of smoke extraction, this modern hood allows for focused light throughout the work area while its careful design adds visual interest to the whole.

112

Painting the walls, cabinets, and doors of a room in one color creates a homogenizing effect that visually amplifies the space and provides a neutral backdrop, allowing the furniture to take center stage.

A-A section

C-C section

B-B section

D-D section

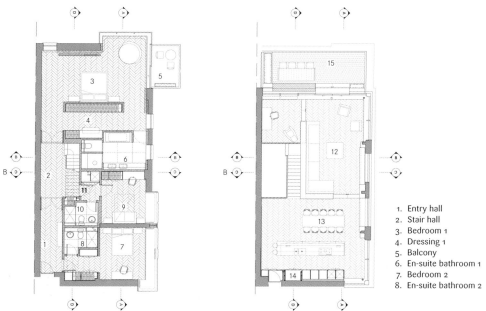

Lower floor plan

Upper floor plan

1. Entry hall
2. Stair hall
3. Bedroom 1
4. Dressing 1
5. Balcony
6. En-suite bathroom 1
7. Bedroom 2
8. En-suite bathroom 2
9. Study bedroom 3
10. En-suite bathroom 3
11. Lobby
12. Sitting
13. Dining
14. Kitchen
15. External terrace

113

The design of the staircase and the railing allows for a visual connection between both floors and for the light coming in from above to give clarity to the entrance corridor.

114

The upholstered panel functions
as a headboard for the bed as well
as a divider for the bedroom and
the dressing room that is located
just behind it. As it is open on both
sides, it favors spatial fluidity and
light entering the wardrobe area.

356 Bermondsey Wall Duplex Penthouse

115

Suspended furniture and sanitary ware, leaving the floor bare, bring visual lightness and a sensation of spaciousness. At the same time, cleaning is much simpler. Design, comfort, and functionality come together.

116

The bench, although less comfortable, can accommodate more guests than if they were sitting on chairs. It is also a good resource as an extra storage area.

Union Square Loft

2,500 sq ft

New York, New York,
United States

**Aamir Khandwala
Interior Design**

© Jacob Snavely

This loft was designed for a couple—two very successful and philanthropic individuals who love to entertain, and who are close friends of the designer—to be their main residence.

The project was a total gut renovation, which allowed it to be absolutely adapted to the needs of the couple, and took approximately one year to complete. The design is sophisticated but unfussy, current but timeless, comfortable for two, but also for entertaining over two hundred guests.

Careful consideration was made in the selection of each detail and to create spaces that reflect the personalities of the clients.

A huge piece by Sadie Benning brings a note of color, filling the space with energy and vitality.

A mural by Shantell Martin is another of the works that are part of the wonderful and diverse collection on display in this loft.

Special attention was paid to the choice
of materials so that they were not only
pleasant to the touch but also easy to
maintain.

117

The glass wall that separates the bedroom from the living area, combined with the wooden door, allows for privacy but without losing the feeling of depth and spatial continuity.

Nob Hill Residence

5,500 sq ft

San Francisco, California,
United States

Dumican Mosey Architects

© Blake Marvin Photography
  Jacob Elliott Photography
  (facade)

A four-story full interior remodel and addition updated this
stately townhouse in Nob Hill with an elegant, modern design.
A sculptural, curved staircase connects the entry level with its
wine and media room to the generous second and third floor
bedroom levels as well as the top floor open kitchen/living/
dining room. The added fourth floor living space takes full
advantage of the incredible views of the Coit Tower, Bay Bridge,
and downtown San Francisco.

Throughout the home, dark walnut detailing, Venetian
plaster walls, and marble bathrooms lend the space a warm,
sophisticated air. The result is a modern yet timeless home.

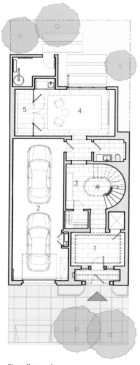

First floor plan

Second floor plan

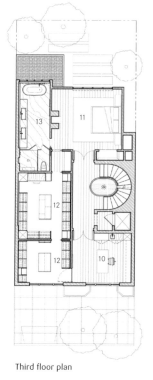

Third floor plan

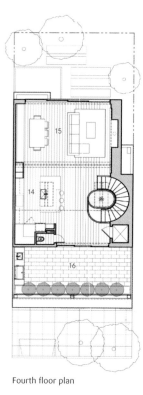

Fourth floor plan

1. Entry
2. Garage
3. Stair hall
4. Media room
5. Wine room
6. Bedroom 1
7. Bedroom 2
8. Guest bedroom suite
9. Laundry
10. Study
11. Master bedroom
12. Master walk-in closet
13. Master bathroom
14. Kitchen
15. Living/dining
16. Outdoor terrace

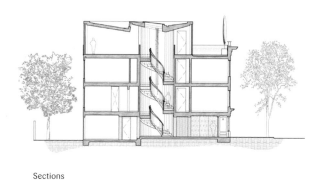

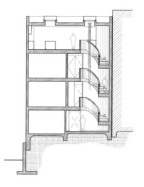

Sections

Past and present coexist in harmony in this house, where on a classical facade that has been rehabilitated, a new modern volume of pure lines rests.

Expansive sliding glass doors allow for
an indoor-outdoor living experience
right in the center of the city.

118

The cellar has been installed on the lower floor so that it does not receive direct light and the product is not altered. It is also an intimate corner in which to enjoy the pleasure of tasting a good wine.

119

The ceiling lamp installed in the upper part of the stairwell provides an ideal and safe illumination while functioning as a decorative element, which, together with the sculptured staircase, creates a spectacular ensemble.

120

The fireplace makes the bedroom more intimate, romantic, and warm. When choosing it, the dimensions of the room, the design style, and its color scheme were taken into account to make the space a harmonious whole.

Art House 2.0

3,600 sq ft

Pound Ridge, New York,
United States

**Carol Kurth Architecture
+ Carol Kurth Interiors**

© Albert Vecerka/Esto

Nestled into a wooded property, this house is a new
construction, modern passive solar house that showcases
the clients' modern art and mid-century modern furniture
collection. The house is an open, airy, gallery-like home that
frames views of the natural woodland setting. The use of
indigenous ashlar, fieldstone, and cedar siding juxtaposes the
home's rectilinear forms and glass expanses.

As the house was designed with views framed to nature, the
clients can enjoy the art of the landscape and ever-changing
display of nature while also reveling in the permanent collection
of art within. Embedded in the woods, the residence is a
tranquil canvas for two art lovers.

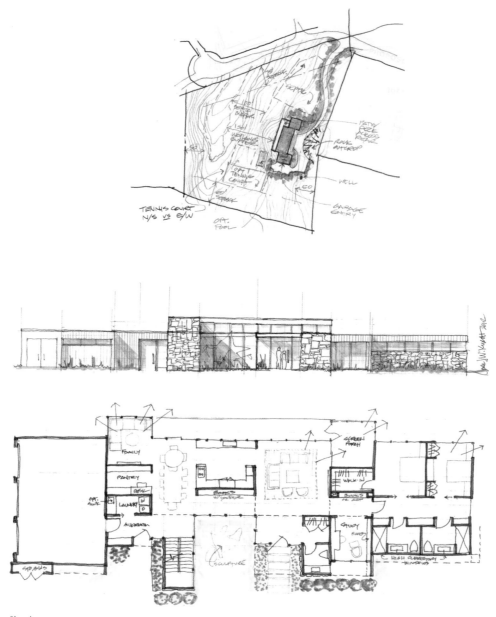

Sketches

Site plan

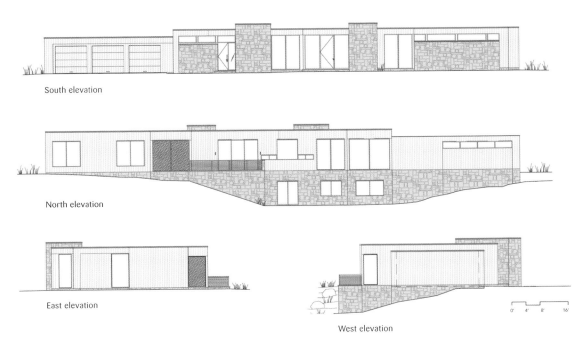

South elevation

North elevation

East elevation

West elevation

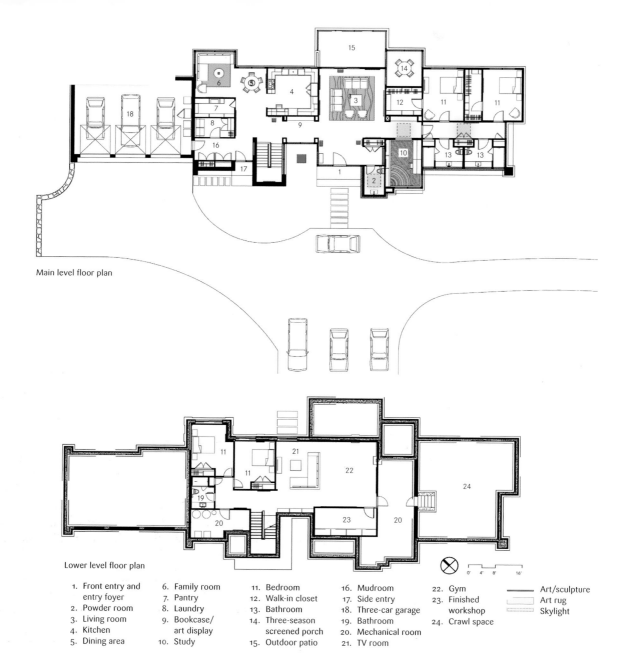

Main level floor plan

Lower level floor plan

1. Front entry and entry foyer
2. Powder room
3. Living room
4. Kitchen
5. Dining area
6. Family room
7. Pantry
8. Laundry
9. Bookcase/ art display
10. Study
11. Bedroom
12. Walk-in closet
13. Bathroom
14. Three-season screened porch
15. Outdoor patio
16. Mudroom
17. Side entry
18. Three-car garage
19. Bathroom
20. Mechanical room
21. TV room
22. Gym
23. Finished workshop
24. Crawl space

—— Art/sculpture
▭ Art rug
▦ Skylight

121

Many of the design elements that the clients loved decades ago stood the test of time and were translated into modern iterations in this new setting of living.

122

Several sculpture niches, inside and out, are designed to focus the views within and further the inside-outside gallery environment.

123

The architect strategically designed space for the owners' extensive art collection during a project phase dedicated specifically to inventory and establishing the art's placement.

The lines of the interior and outdoors
blur with a gallery-like environment,
creating a backdrop for their enjoyment
of nature, art, and books.

The surrounding woods give the home's interior a feeling of being in a treehouse. The architect designed the stone facade with recessed mortar to mimic the effect of natural dry-laid stone walls indigenous to the area. These walls contrast with the wood and glass composition.

Fancy Pants

2,750 sq ft

Chicago, Illinois, United States

PROjECT

© Chris Bradley

After crossing the front door of this apartment, one cannot help but be surprised—not only by the spectacular views over the Chicago River, but by the magic of the atmosphere created by the PROjECT team. The owners, who usually live on the outskirts of the city, wanted a pied-à-terre in the center where they could feel like they were in a boutique hotel. The result is unbeatable: an apartment with an avant-garde urban style, where you can relax comfortably while enjoying the infinite views it offers, and with many creative solutions to achieve the highest standard of comfort and quality.

124

To amplify the condo's east-, south-, and west-facing views, low-profile furniture was chosen, including a showstopping, tufted glazed linen sectional for the living room and automatic shades to let the light in at the push of a button.

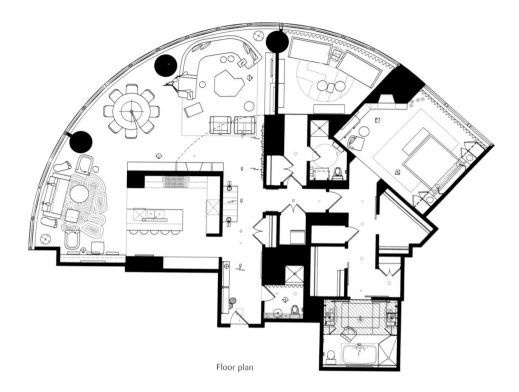

Floor plan

An open living and dining area, two
bedrooms, two bathrooms, a toilet,
and a kitchen that a Michelin-starred
chef would love make up this dream
apartment in downtown Chicago.

125

The wonky angles of the layout might have posed a challenge, but the designer saw them as opportunities worthy of accentuating. In the dining room, she opted for a round table with a slitted concrete top by James De Wulf that's welcoming from all sides.

126

To create a more welcoming atmosphere during Chicago's polar winters, two unvented fireplaces with blackened steel frames were installed in the dining room and master bedroom.

127

Finding creative storage solutions was another essential goal that was stylishly solved with custom-made oak cabinets with a dark finish in both the master bedroom and the dining room.

To give a touch of color and exclusivity to the bathroom, a paper from the Black Crow Studio was chosen, which gives the impression of having been painted in watercolor.

Bonner

1,884 sq ft

Manly, New South Wales,
Australia

Smart Design Studio

© Ross Honeysett

Updated planning, finishes, and furniture revitalised this apartment within a 1970's modernist block.

With sweeping views of Manly and Sydney Harbour, the new interior design respects and blends with the era of the building, tailoring it to suit the new owner's needs. A classic yet luxurious palette of gray travertine, white linen, and book matched flamed myrtle veneer complements the simple forms and modernist planning. Custom fittings and clever detailing combined with signature curves complete the picture.

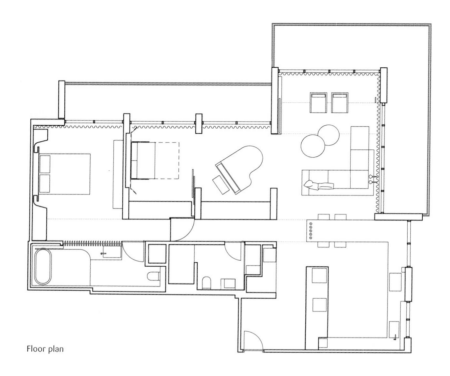

Floor plan

Living spaces and bedrooms are
organized along the view facade, and
the wet rooms form a single block
accessed off a circulation gallery. The
master bedroom remains where it was,
while the second bedroom, furnished
with an elegant sofa bed, opens to
become part of the living space.

The television is outlined by a sinuous
steel frame that, much like everything
else, plays a functional role rather than
a merely decorative one.

The modernist approach extends to the lighting and furniture. The paired Arne Jacobson lamps and Bertoia stools are the most overt genre references.

128

Heavily patterned flamed myrtle veneer cladding the joinery provides a counterpoint to the three-meter-long cantilevered Corian island bench and the plain white ceilings.

129

Strips of plush black and terra-
cotta carpet add interest to the
expanse of gray travertine tiles
and soft flooring.

130

The sculptural wood-lined walls integrate joinery and conceal services to create a refined space with warmth and personality.

131

In the master en suite, the custom Corian basin and sculptural bath contrast with the charcoal glass walls, reinforcing the theme of luxurious modernism that runs throughout.

Fresh and serene, this is a Park Avenue loft with a decidedly downtown feel. The space is refined and elegant but also modern and relaxed. Sculptural lighting, such as the Lariat 3 by Apparatus Studio and String Lights by Michael Anastassiades, adds drama and emphasizes the high ceilings, whilst oversized artwork and bold textiles, such as the Diego rug by Eskayel, add color and depth. Iconic mid-century pieces inspired by the designs of Hans Wegner, Poul Kjaerholm, and Eero Saarinen are paired with more contemporary custom millwork, such as the black and brass floating wall shelves, floating upholstered bench, and marble and black oak nightstands. A curated collection of accessories in a mix of sizes, shapes, and materials completes the scheme.

Fresh and Serene on Park Avenue South

1,600 sq ft

New York, New York, United States

The New Design Project

© Alan Gastelum

Floor plan

1. Living room
2. Bathroom
3. Dining area
4. Kitchen
5. Master bedroom
6. Bedroom
7. Closet
8. Powder

132

The black wall takes on a great prominence and creates an interesting contrast with the white. In addition, the color black helps to create a feeling of depth.

133

Taking advantage of the column, a wall has been erected that serves as a bench for the dining area. In this way the column is integrated into the decorative composition without giving the impression of being in the middle and also serves as a room divider.

134

A bench to read, look, listen to
music, relax . . . with a view always
by the window. It is a great idea
to take advantage of the space of
a window to create a unique and
magical corner.

135

The area around the sink, which
is more exposed to splashes,
has been covered with the same
marble as the countertop, as the
wallpaper usually deteriorates due
to the water.

Sunny Isles

3,000 sq ft
Miami, Florida, United States

Sanchez+Coleman

© Ken Hayden

The clients, a couple with two teenage children, were looking for a fresh, family-friendly space where they could receive visitors, with the latest technology and an interior design as striking as the ocean views from their terraces. To add interest and dimension to the living area, which was originally a basic white box, the walls were rebuilt to give the space a faceted three-dimensional effect: the architecture was changed, and the walls were turned into large art pieces.

A scheme of Klein blue and bright yellow was used to play with the black and white that imbues the entire home with energy. The furniture includes mid-century icons and customized contemporary pieces. Now, full of art and ingenuity, this once ordinary apartment has become a masterpiece.

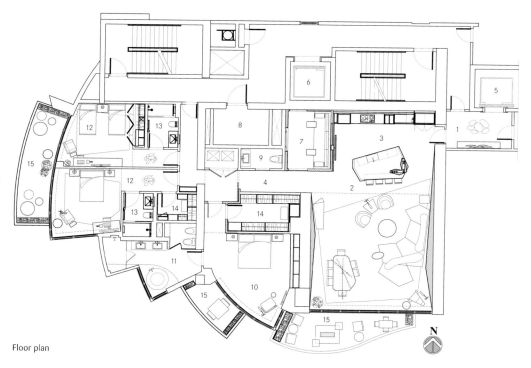

Floor plan

1. Foyer
2. Great room
3. Kitchen
4. Hallway/gallery
5. Public elevator
6. Service elevator
7. Den
8. Mechanical room
9. Powder room
10. Master bedroom
11. Master bathroom
12. Bedroom
13. Bathroom
14. Walk-in closet
15. Terrace

N

In the dining area, a suite of Cappellini chairs surrounds a custom Angela Adams table. The wall sculpture is by Matthew Hawtin, the light fixture is from David Weeks Studio, and the sculpture atop the pedestal is by Alberto Cavalieri.

136

The column has been cleverly used to frame the kitchen area. From it comes a pristine Corian island that serves as a breakfast bar or a casual lunch and work area.

The spectacular work of art "Cercle Bleu" signed by the master Manuel Merida, which on the blue glass wall could remind us of a beautiful full moon night, becomes the focal point of the kitchen area.

137

The upholstered wall, the sofas full of cushions, and the carpet are enough to soundproof this audiovisual room, whose aesthetics, with Klein blue as the absolute protagonist, are spectacular. The wall art is by Saul Galavais.

A blue wall sculpture by Matthew Hawtin and a console from the Future Perfect activate this corner.

138

An all-white bedroom doesn't have to be boring or monotonous. The use of different materials creates incredible contrasts of textures that enrich the space and are enhanced by the abundant light that enters through the window.

139

The terrace must keep an aesthetic in accordance with the house. Thus, on the terrace overlooking the living room, some armchairs from Room & Board and a chariot from Fermob form an ideal set to enjoy a moment of reading or a pleasant gathering in the sun.

Bonham Strand 1

1,937 + 1,615 sq ft
Hong Kong, China

Peggy Bels

© Eugene Chan

Hidden on the fourth floor of a nondescript building in the bustling heart of Sheung Wan, this apartment becomes a serene oasis in the midst of so much hustle and bustle.

After a seven-month renovation process, four apartments were converted into a spacious contemporary, minimalist apartment with a color palette of muted grays and black that is still warm and inviting.

A diversity of souvenirs from the owners' travels are interspersed with an enviable collection of modern art and sculptural design furniture from the mid-twentieth century, adding a touch of personal and anthropological history in a minimalist, elegant space with a certain air of sophistication.

The palette of materials based on subtly
textured concrete, ashen metals, and
wood is extended throughout the house.

140

Natural light, which is a key point in the design, enters in abundance through two skylights installed in the living area that allow daylight to penetrate deep into the interior.

141

To keep the open kitchen fuss-free, two metal sliding doors were added to hide the sink area, blending in with the rest of the wall. The oblong concrete kitchen table acts as the social fulcrum of the apartment.

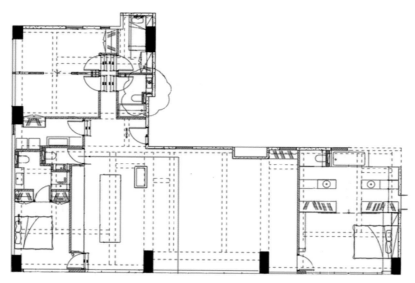

Floor plan

The apartment has four bedrooms—a master bedroom, a guest bedroom, and two children's bedrooms—a large open living area, and a terrace almost as large as the apartment.

The master and guest bedrooms afford
views of the expansive terrace.

142

The two contiguous children's bedrooms are separated by a sliding door, which allows for the creation of a playful hideaway when combined or two separate private retreats when the sliding door is closed.

The windows allow nature to enter
the bathrooms, adding freshness and
a touch of color.

The terrace is perfect for playing, socializing, or relaxing. Considered an extension of the interior, it houses a lounge, a bar, a dining area, and a grass-covered area, ideal for children to play.

Art-House Residence

3,340 sq ft

Melbourne, Victoria, Australia

Lilian H Weinreich Architects

© Lilian H Weinreich Architects
  High Q Renders

This serene modern townhouse supports the creative lifestyle of a famed young artist. The residence occupies a prized urban site of two narrow lots that front a green public square. Although constrained by height limitations and mandated setbacks, the design achieves a spacious three-story dwelling by using the site's gentle slope.

The residence's plan arranges program elements into two zones. One accommodates the artist, and the second contains a two-bedroom rental apartment. Both zones work independently but can combine seamlessly as a single dwelling.

Evincing close attention to detail, the design lies at the intersection of functional planning, spatial resolution, aesthetic detailing, and artistic display.

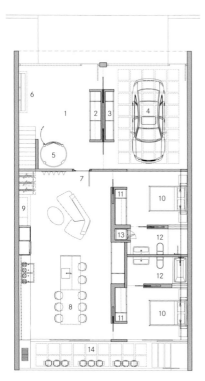

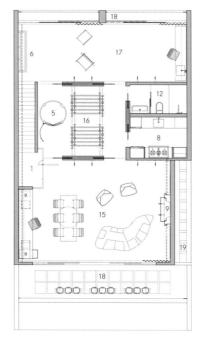

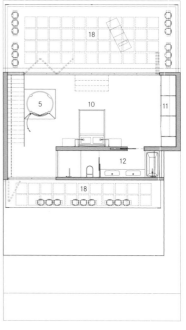

Entry/first level

Second floor

Third floor

0 2 4   8   16FT

1. Entry
2. Coats/storage
3. Tools/recycle bins
4. Car park
5. Glass elevator
6. Motorized art hoist
7. Renter's unit
8. Kitchen
9. Gas fireplace
10. Bedroom
11. Closet
12. Bathroom
13. Laundry closet
14. Sunken garden
15. Artist's unit office/
    meeting/library
16. Lateral art storage
17. Artist's studio
18. Exterior terrace
19. Skylight/operable
    windows

The artist's zone occupies the second and third levels and consists of a high-ceilinged studio and office, client meeting/gallery area, art storage, and sleeping quarters.

143

The concrete floor has an industrial appearance, but with a point of sophistication that makes it fit into any environment. It becomes a comfortable base to give character. It creates a pleasant sensation of continuity as it has no joints, which visually expands the spaces.

144

A glass elevator addresses future accessibility needs, and a custom motorized hoist system facilitates the transportation of large-scale artwork from the twelve-foot-high studio level to the large garage below.

145

In order to give more warmth to the artist's private area, the nobility of the wood has been used to clad the gently sloped ceiling in both the bedroom and the bathroom and also creates a beautiful contrast of colors and textures.

Summit New York

PH Unit C = 1,908 sq ft
Studio Unit H = 484 sq ft
Studio Unit C = 599 sq ft

New York, New York,
United States

**Lemay+Escobar Architecture,
D.P.C.**

© Qualls Benson
 Inessa Binenbaum

With its forty-three floors in downtown Manhattan, this is an unprecedented project in the city. Aiming at a very high-income target audience, Lemay+Escobar designed more than 400 residential units, two levels of luxury penthouses, and three floors of exceptionally well-designed spaces, such as a private club for residents. The interiors are sophisticated, with eclectic yet harmonious design elements that are both contemporary and timeless.

By the time the residents arrive home, they are living in an elegant space away from the everyday world—a space that embodies sophistication, calm, and softness: in short, a private oasis.

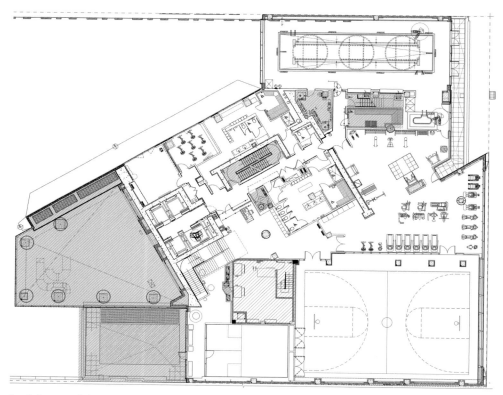

Fourth floor overall plan

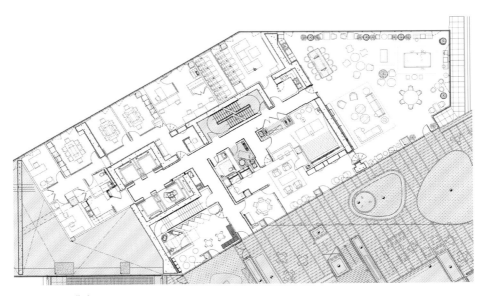

Sixth floor overall plan

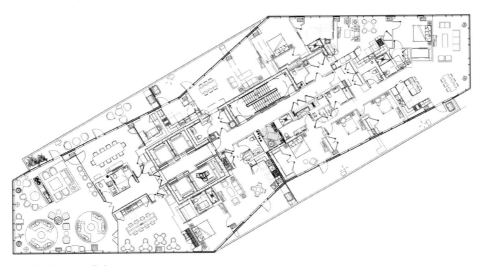

Forty-first floor overall plan

146

The indirect lighting is perfect for any time of day and fits into every room. Placed on the shelves, aside from creating a warm and intimate atmosphere, it also serves to accentuate the objects the shelves contain and give them prominence.

147

Being surrounded by asphalt and the imposing buildings of the Big Apple, including some plants in the living areas is a good option, since they act as living sculptures, adding a natural artistic brushstroke that transmits life and energy.

148

Putting the dining area in front of large windows is a great choice. You will have natural light and enjoy the views while eating, and it will provide a very relaxing feeling of openness to the exterior.

In line with NYC's environmental protection standards, the project is energy-efficient. Its materials, appliances, and internal systems correspond with several LEED criteria.

Each space was designed with a palette of naturally rich materials, well-crafted details, and curated design elements.

149

The free-standing bath projects a sense of luxury and well-being and by its design becomes the focal point of the room. Since it is also placed in front of the window, the bathing experience is unbeatable.

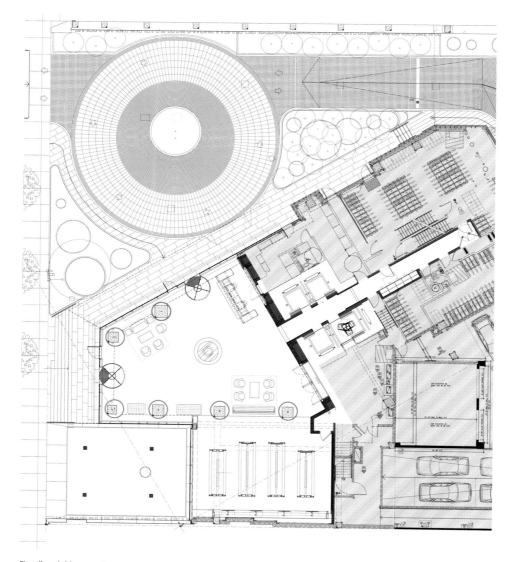

First floor lobby overall

150

Without being ostentatious, the towering lobby serves as a transformational corridor, greeting residents with a breathtaking display of modern elegance.

DIRECTORY

Aamir Khandwala Interior Design
New York, New York, United States
aamirkhandwala.com

Abrils Studio
Terrassa, Spain
Breda, Netherlands
abrilsstudio.com

Alexander Butler Design Services
New York, New York, United States
abdsnyc.com

Aviram-Kushmirski
Tel Aviv, Israel
oshridana.com

Axis Mundi
New York, New York, United States
axismundi.com

B Interior
New York, New York, United States
binterior.com

Belzberg Architects
Santa Monica, California, United States
belzbergarchitects.com

Boffi
Lentate sul Seveso, Italy
boffi.com

**Carol Kurth Architecture +
Carol Kurth Interiors**
Bedford, New York, United States
carolkurtharchitects.com

D'Aquino Monaco
New York, New York, United States
daquinomonaco.com

Diego Revollo Arquitetura
São Paulo, Brazil
www.diegorevollo.com.br

dSPACE Studio
Chicago, Illinois, United States
www.dspacestudio.com

DKOR Interiors
Miami, Florida, United States
dkorinteriors.com

Dumican Mosey Architects
San Francisco, California, United States
dumicanmosey.com

Filoramo Talsma Architecture
Chicago, Illinois, United States
filoramotalsma.com

Fiona Lynch
Melbourne, Victoria, Australia
fionalynch.com.au

FORMstudio
London, United Kingdom
formstudio.co.uk

Hariri & Hariri Architecture
New York, New York, United States
haririandhariri.com

John Lum Architecture
San Francisco, California, United States
johnlumarchitecture.com

Kelli Richards Designs
Montreal, Quebec, Canada
kellirichardsdesigns.com

Lemay+Escobar Architecture, D.P.C.
New York, New York, United States
lemayescobar.com

Lilian H Weinreich Architects
New York, New York, United States
www.weinreich-architects.com

Messana O'Rorke
New York, New York, United States
messanaororke.com

MLK Studio
Los Angeles, California, United States
mlkstudio.com

Peggy Bels
Hong Kong, China
Paris, France
peggybels.com

PROjECT
Chicago, Illinois, United States
projectinteriors.com

Robert Bailey Interiors
Vancouver, British Columbia, Canada
robertbaileyinteriors.ca

**Ruiz Velázquez architecture & design
Madrid, Spain**
Dubai, United Arab Emirates
ruizvelazquez.com

Sanchez+Coleman
Miami, Florida, United States
sanchezcolemanstudio.com

Smart Design Studio
Sydney, New South Wales, Australia
smartdesignstudio.com

Studio RODA
Miami, Florida, United States
studioroda.net

SPF:architects
Los Angeles, California, United States
spfa.com

Studio Gild
Chicago, Illinois, United States
Los Angeles, California, United States
studiogild.com

The New Design Project
New York, New York, United States
thenewdesignproject.com